GECKOS
OTHER
& BEAD
ANIMALS

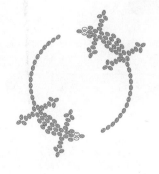

Drew Wilkens

Bead Man

Press

Issaquah, Washington

ISBN 0-9663591-0-0

All illustrations by Drew Wilkens

Printed in the USA

First printing February, 1998

Contents

Introduction

Geckos and other bead animals is a
project book inspired by the children
of the Pacific Northwest. I was introduced
to the bead Gecko in 1997 but its roots
are found in the cities and towns of Washington, Oregon and Alaska since 1995.

Bead Animals are a fun and imaginative
activity. You can hang them from your
backpacks or trade them with your
friends. If fun is not enough, beading is a
great developer of fine motor skills.

This book is presented in several stages.
You will learn a how to create a "stitch",
then be shown different projects using
that stitch. To keep it fun and challenging,
each project is a little harder than the
first.

Have a great time with this book and keep
art in your life.

- Drew Wilkens
"The Bead Man"

Getting Started
Beads

If you are just learning, it is a good idea to start out with large beads like "Crow" or "Pony" Beads. Pony beads are 9mm in diameter and have a large hole. They can be made of glass or plastic. Plastic beads are affordable, light weight and are easily found in bead or craft stores. As your skills develop, try smaller beads like 6mm, No. 6 seed beads or tiny seed beads like 10 or 11.

 9mm

 6mm

No.6

No.10

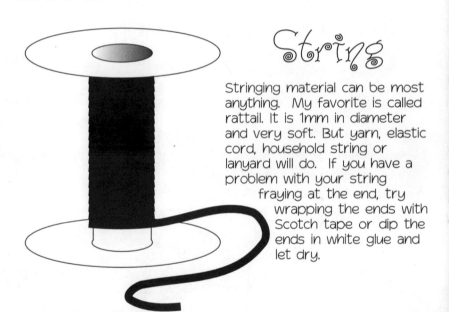

String

Stringing material can be most anything. My favorite is called rattail. It is 1mm in diameter and very soft. But yarn, elastic cord, household string or lanyard will do. If you have a problem with your string fraying at the end, try wrapping the ends with Scotch tape or dip the ends in white glue and let dry.

Key Ring

Geckos are a backpack must! Add a key ring and you are on your way.

Basic Stitch – Body

There are several types of stitches used in this book. All of the projects require the most basic called the body stitch..

STEP 1

String the number of beads necessary for the first row. Fold the string in half, and let the beads slide to the middle

STEP 2

Place beads for the next row on side B of the string (the side you start with does not affect the design)

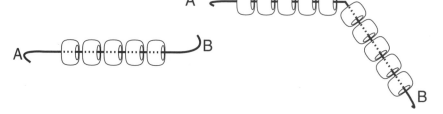

STEP 3

Thread side A off your string through the beads on side B going the opposite way.

STEP 4

Pull tight.

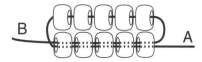

STEP 5

Repeat steps 2, 3 and 4. That is all there is to it.

Basic Stitch - Leg

There is variation in the leg stitch, usually the number of toes. The following example is from the three toed gecko.

STEP 1

Place 6 beads on your string (3 beads for the leg, 3 beads for the toe).

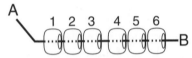

STEP 2

Using the same side of the string (B) skip beads 4-5-6 and thread wire back thru 3-2-1 and pull tight.

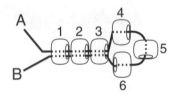

The leg may be too far from the body. To move it closer, grab the center toe bead (#5) and pull side B. This will slide the leg closer to the main segment.

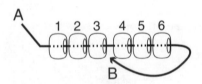

Basic Stitch - Ear

The ear stitch can also be used to create a flipper.

STEP 1

To create the ear, place 8 beads on side **B**, of your string.

STEP 2

Bring the string back thru the beads by skipping bead #8 and threading thru, in order, #6 then #7. Pull tight.

STEP 3

Thread thru beads #4, then #5. Pull tight.

STEP 4

Thread thru beads #2, then #3. Pull tight.

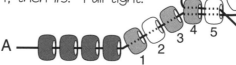

STEP 5

Thread thru beads #1. Pull tight and continue the pattern using the body stitch and leg stitch.

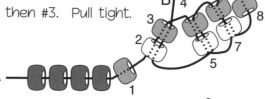

Review:
Threading order
1 - 2 - 3 - 4 - 5 -
6 - 7 - 8 - 6 - 7 -
4 - 5 - 2 - 3 - 1

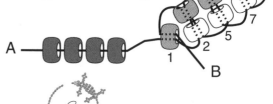

Basic Stitch - Tail

Although the tail is made with a simple 1 bead body stitch, it is often a point of confusion.

STEP 1
When you reach the tail, place 1 bead on side A of the wire.

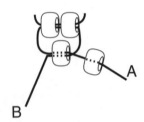

STEP 2
Thread wire B the opposing direction

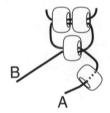

STEP 3
Pull tight and repeat.

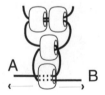

 Inchworm

The Inchworm is a great first project. To make the inchworm, we will be learning the "body stitch".

STEP 1

Create the first row by placing three beads in the center of your string

A ⟨⟩⟨⟩⟨⟩ B

STEP 2

Place four beads (second row) on the **B** side of your string.

A ⟨⟩⟨⟩⟨⟩ ⬛⬛⬛⬛ B

STEP 3

Take side **A** of your string and thread thru four beads on side **B**.

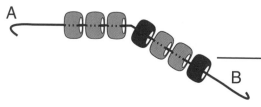

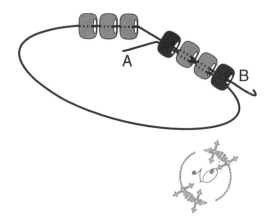

STEP 4

Pull the two ends tight. This is called a "body stitch".

STEP 5

Refer to the **layout** for the next row. Place three beads on string **A**.

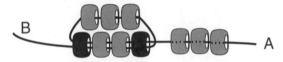

STEP 6

Thread side **B** thru the beads.

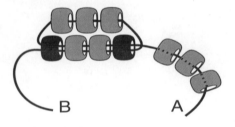

STEP 7

Pull tight. Continue using the body stitch for the entire pattern

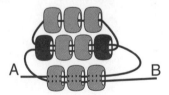

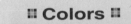

Tip

If you are having difficulty with your string fraying at the end, dip the ends in Elmer's Glue or wrap the ends with tape

Factoid:

The inchworm, or measuring worm, is the larva of the moth family Geometridae (from the Greek "earth measurer"). Crawling is accomplished by pulling the hind end forward and then extending the front in a series of vertical loops.

▦ Colors ▦

◼ Black	(2)
◻ Lt Green	(31)
◻ Yellow	(25)
▬ String	6 ft

Rattlesnake

"SHAKE"

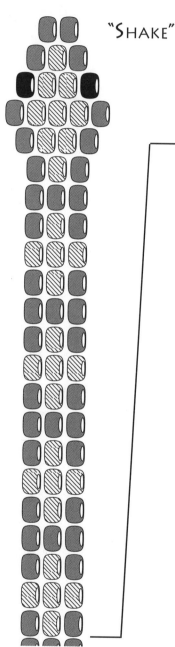

Continued

Factoid:
The eastern diamondback, can grow up to eight feet long. The rattlesnake can detect temperature differences of thousandths of a degree, allowing it to strike accurately in total darkness.

Body stitch

:: **Colors** ::	
Black	(2)
Brown	(57)
Red	(39)
White	(10)
String	8 ft

Letters

Write your name, your school, even a favorite sports team in your favorite colors.

use the
letter
guides
on
pages
41 - 44

Requires 1.5ft
string per letter

Wrist Watch

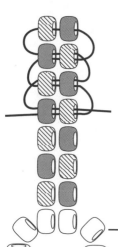

STEP 1
Begin the watch using the "body stitch"

STEP 2
When you reach the watch dial, place three beads on side **A** and 3 beads on side **B**.

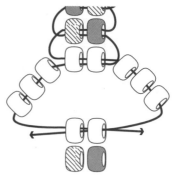

STEP 3
Continue with the body stitch. When you complete the last row, thread the string thru the beads in the first row and tie a knot..

The watch can also be made using elastic cord.

Factoid:
The most accurate time-piece is the atomic clock located in Colorado. Atomic clocks may be accurate to within 1 second in many thousands of years.

Body stitch

:: Colors ::	
Blue	(14)
Purple	(14)
Red	(2)
Yellow	(10)
String	3 ft

Christmas Tree

STEP 1

Start with the star (1 white bead) in the middle of your string. Place 2 beads from row 2 on side B. Thread side A thru both beads.

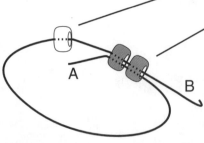

STEP 2

Pull both ends tight. Follow the tree layout adding one additional bead in each row.

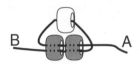

STEP 3

To finish, tie a simple knot at the trunk.

Factoid:

The Germans were the first to decorate trees they called Paradise Trees. Around Christmas time the family would decorate it with wafers, and later cookies, candles, and other forms of decoration.

Body Stitch

## Colors ##	
Brown	(4)
Green	(46)
Any Color	(8)
White	(1)
String	4 ft

Jack o' Lantern

Start at the top of the Jack 'O Lantern with two beads, follow the layout using the "body stitch"

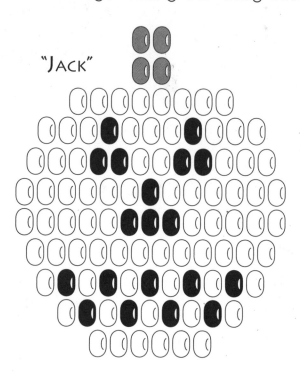

"JACK"

Factoid:

Now a children's holiday, Halloween was originally a Celtic festival for the dead, celebrated on the last day of the Celtic year, Oct. 31. Until recent times in some parts of Europe, it was believed that on this night witches and warlocks flew abroad; and huge bonfires were built to ward off these malevolent spirits.

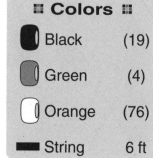

Body Stitch

▦ **Colors** ▦	
▉ Black	(19)
◖ Green	(4)
◗ Orange	(76)
▬ String	6 ft

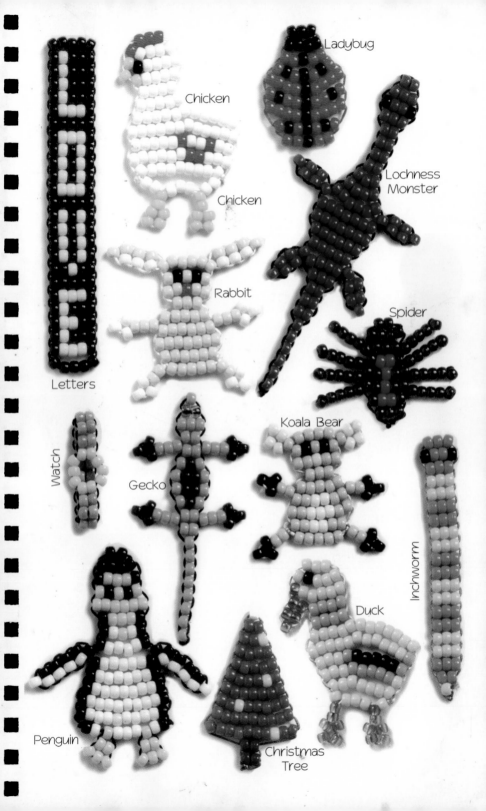

Ladybug

Chicken

Lochness Monster

Chicken

Rabbit

Spider

Letters

Watch

Gecko

Koala Bear

Inchworm

Penguin

Christmas Tree

Duck

Ladybug

Factoid:

Finding a ladybug is considered good luck. In the garden they eat aphids, scale insects, and other plant pests. They are a great gardening alternative to dangerous pesticides.

"JUNE"

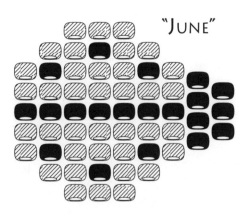

Body stitch

▦ **Colors** ▦	
⬛ Black	(20)
🔲 Red	(38)
▬ String	4 ft

Happy Face

Body stitch

▦ **Colors** ▦	
⬛ Black	(8)
⬜ Yellow	(84)
▬ String	6 ft

17

Gecko

The Gecko will teach you how to create a **"leg stitch"**.

"HILO"

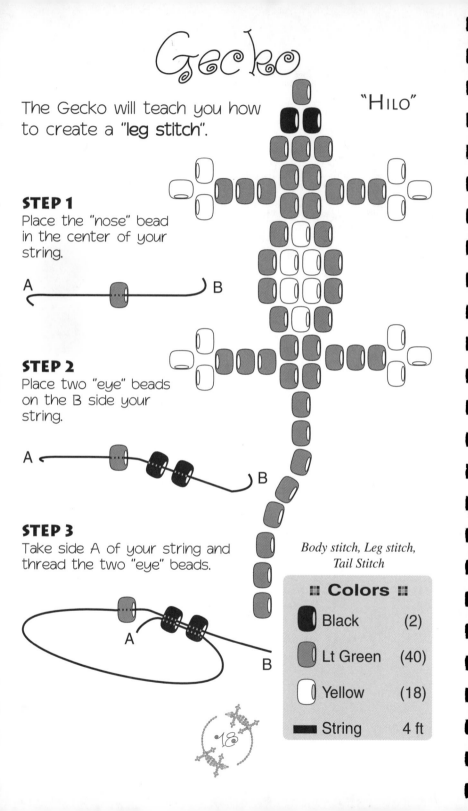

STEP 1
Place the "nose" bead in the center of your string.

A   B

STEP 2
Place two "eye" beads on the B side your string.

A   B

STEP 3
Take side A of your string and thread the two "eye" beads.

A

B

Body stitch, Leg stitch, Tail Stitch

▦ Colors ▦

Black	(2)
Lt Green	(40)
Yellow	(18)
String	4 ft

STEP 4

Pull the two ends tight. This is the "body stitch" used in previous projects.

STEP 5

Refer to the layout for the next row. Place three beads on string A. Repeat the steps in the "body stitch" and continue until you reach the legs.

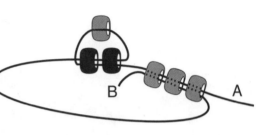

STEP 6

To make a "leg stitch", place 6 beads on side B.

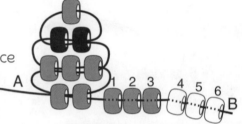

STEP 7

Skip beads #6,#5,#4 and come back thru #3,#2 and #1. Pull tight. Repeat steps 6 & 7 to make the leg on side A.

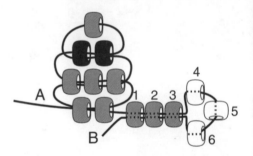

STEP 8

Follow the layout to complete your gecko. The tail is made with 1 bead using the body stitch.

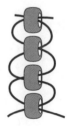

Skunk

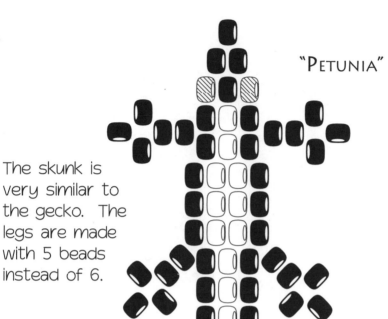

"PETUNIA"

The skunk is very similar to the gecko. The legs are made with 5 beads instead of 6.

The tail is made the same way as the body..

Body stitch, Leg stitch

▦ Colors ▦

▉ Black	(53)
▢ White	(17)
▨ Blue	(2)
▬ String	4 ft

Factoid:

Skunks, often mistakenly called polecats, are members of the weasel family. They are well known for the repulsive-smelling spray they eject from the base of the tail when disturbed.

Bullfrog

"Toro"

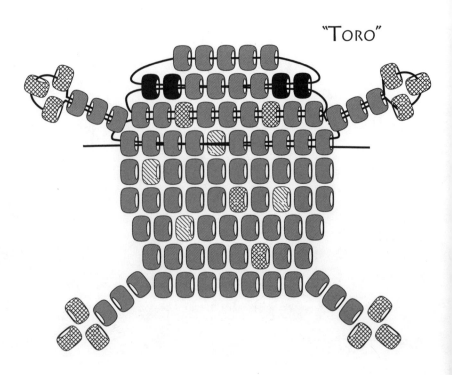

Factoid:

The bullfrog grows to 8 inches in body length. The male's loud, bellowing voice establishes a territory, and defending males may engage in pushing or wrestling matches with intruding bullfrogs. The bullfrog matures slowly, usually taking about five years to become a full adult, and may live for up to 16 years.

Body stitch, Leg stitch

▦ **Colors** ▦	
▌Black	(4)
▌Lt Green	(76)
▧ Yellow	(4)
▨ Dk. Green	(16)
▬ String	7 ft

Turtle

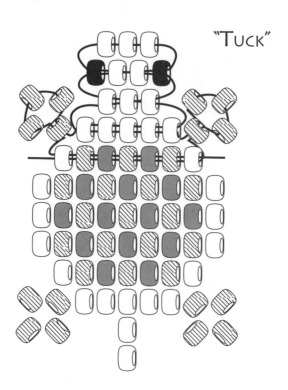

"TUCK"

Factoid:

Turtles range in size from an average of 4 1/2 inches and a few ounces in the bog turtle, to 8ft and 1,985lbs in the leatherback turtle.

Body stitch, Leg stitch

▦ Colors ▦

◼ Black	(2)
▢ Lt Green	(30)
▨ Md. Green	(33)
◼ Dk Green	(14)
▬ String	5ft

Alligator

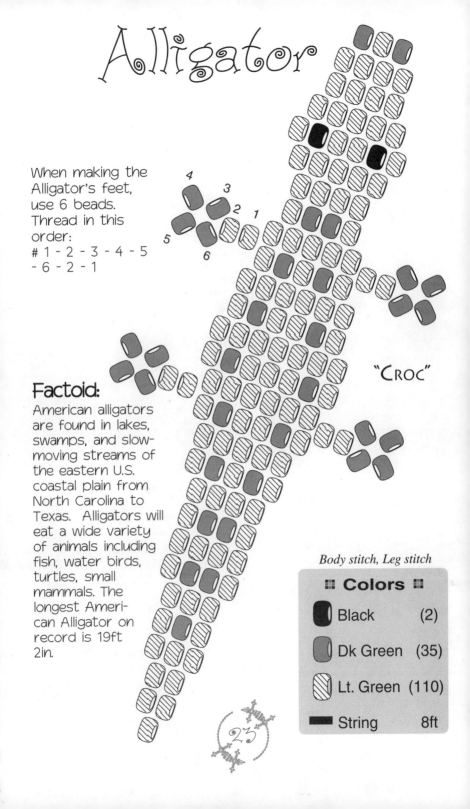

When making the Alligator's feet, use 6 beads. Thread in this order:
\# 1 - 2 - 3 - 4 - 5 - 6 - 2 - 1

4
3
2
1
5
6

"Croc"

Factoid:

American alligators are found in lakes, swamps, and slow-moving streams of the eastern U.S. coastal plain from North Carolina to Texas. Alligators will eat a wide variety of animals including fish, water birds, turtles, small mammals. The longest American Alligator on record is 19ft 2in.

Body stitch, Leg stitch

▦ Colors ▦	
Black	(2)
Dk Green	(35)
Lt. Green	(110)
String	8ft

23

Bead Person

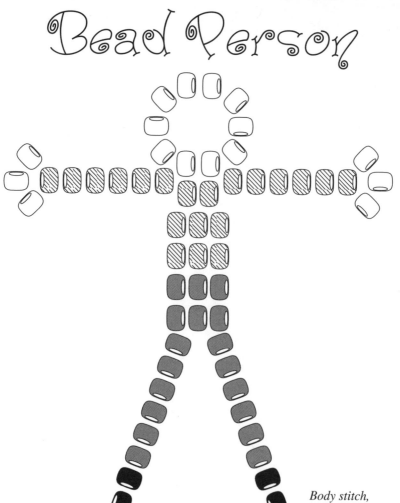

*Body stitch,
Leg stitch*

STEP 1
Place 8 beads on the center of
your string.

A   B

▦ Colors ▦

◯ Yellow	(16)
▨ Red	(20)
◼ Blue	(18)
◼ Brown	(4)
▬ String	4ft

STEP 2
Place two beads on the B side your string

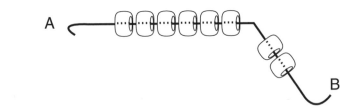

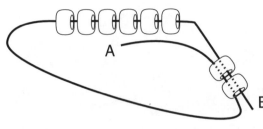

STEP 3
Take side A of your string and thread the two beads.

STEP 4
Pull the two ends tight to form a circle

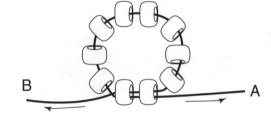

STEP 5
Using techniques found in other projects create the arms of your bead person. (Arms see Gecko; Legs see spider)

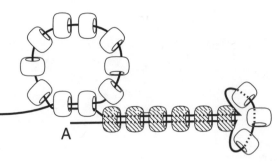

Koala Bear

STEP 1

Start the Koala by placing 4 beads on the center of your string.

"SHEILA"

STEP 2

To create the ear, place 5 beads on side **B**.

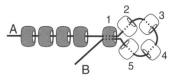

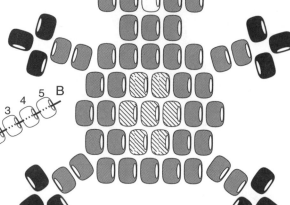

STEP 3

Thread the end of side **B**, thru bead #1 and pull tight.

Factoid:

The koala is not a bear but a marsupial mammal. Koalas are found only in the eucalyptus forests of eastern Australia.

Body stitch, Leg stitch

▓ **Colors** ▓	
■ Black	(14)
■ Dk Brown	(46)
▢ Pink	(9)
▨ Lt Brown	(7)
▬ String	5ft

STEP 4

Repeat steps 2 & 3 on side **A** of your string. Create the next row using the "body stitch"

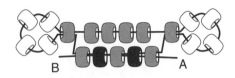

STEP 5

To make the "leg stitch", place 5 beads on side A of the string. Using the same side (A) skip beads 3-4-5 and thread back through beads 2-1.

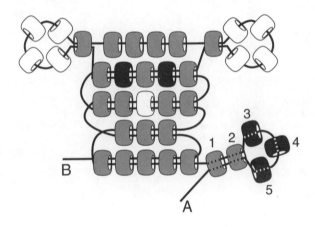

STEP 6

Repeat step 5 using side B of the string. Continue following the pattern using the body stitch and leg stitch.

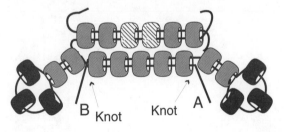

Mouse

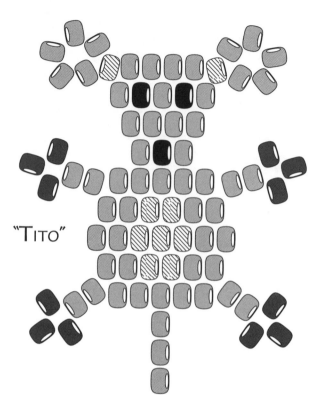

"TITO"

STEP 1

The mouse is made the same way as the koala bear. There are differences in the pattern. The ears are 1 bead larger and the tail is added

Factoid:

A great pet, mice have been an important part of our scientific research.

Body stitch, Leg stitch, Tail Stitch

:: **Colors** ::	
● Black	(3)
● Dk Brown	(13)
▨ Pink	(9)
◻ Grey	(62)
▬ String	5ft

Spider

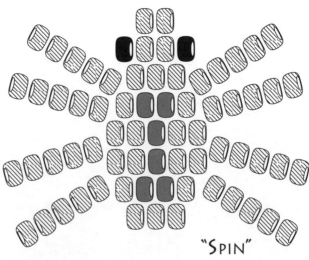

"SPIN"

STEP 1 - STRAIGHT LEG STITCH

To make the straight legs of the spider, place 5 beads on your string

STEP 2

Skip bead #5 and thread back thru 4 - 3 - 2 - 1.

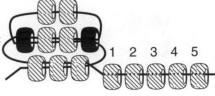

1 2 3 4 5

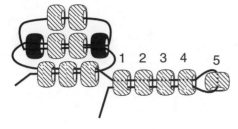

1 2 3 4 5

Factoid:

More than 30,000 species of spiders are found on every continent except Antarctica.

Body stitch, Leg stitch

■■ Colors ■■	
■ Black	(2)
▨ Dk Blue	(62)
▢ Red	(6)
▬ String	5ft

Bunny

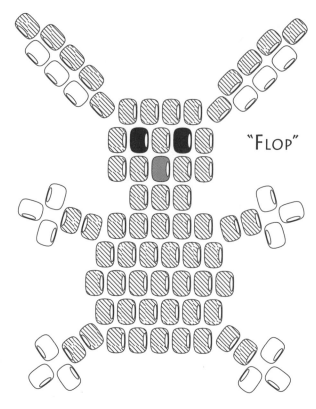

"Flop"

STEP 1

Start the Bunny by placing 4 beads on the center of your string.

A ——⬡⬡⬡⬡—— B

Factoid:

The pygmy rabbit is the smallest rabbit, just 10 in long. The largest is the swamp rabbit, up to 21 in long.

Body stitch, Leg stitch, Ear Stitch

▓ Colors ▓	
⬛ Black	(2)
🔴 Red	(1)
⬡ Pink	(61)
⬜ White	(18)
▬ String	6 ft

STEP 2

To create the ear, place 8 beads on side **B**, of your string.

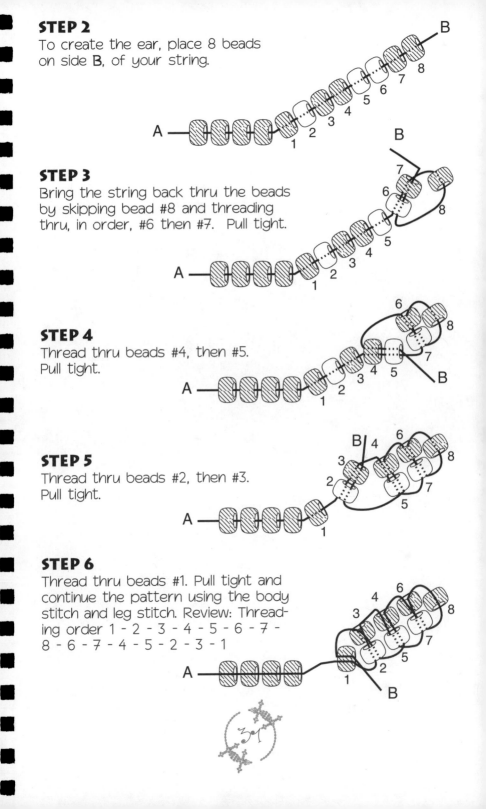

STEP 3

Bring the string back thru the beads by skipping bead #8 and threading thru, in order, #6 then #7. Pull tight.

STEP 4

Thread thru beads #4, then #5. Pull tight.

STEP 5

Thread thru beads #2, then #3. Pull tight.

STEP 6

Thread thru beads #1. Pull tight and continue the pattern using the body stitch and leg stitch. Review: Threading order 1 - 2 - 3 - 4 - 5 - 6 - 7 - 8 - 6 - 7 - 4 - 5 - 2 - 3 - 1

Hound Dog

Start at the top of the head by placing 5 beads in the middle of the string. Make the ears using the stitch demonstrated in the Bunny instructions.

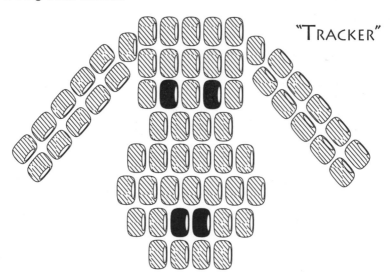

"TRACKER"

Ear

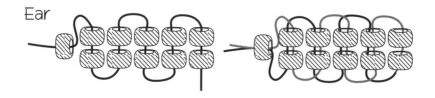

Factoid:

A dog's most important sense is that of smell. Tracking dogs, like the hound, have large ears that help gather the scent to their noses.

Body stitch, Leg stitch, Ear Stitch

▓ **Colors** ▓	
Black	(4)
Brown	(60)
String	5 ft

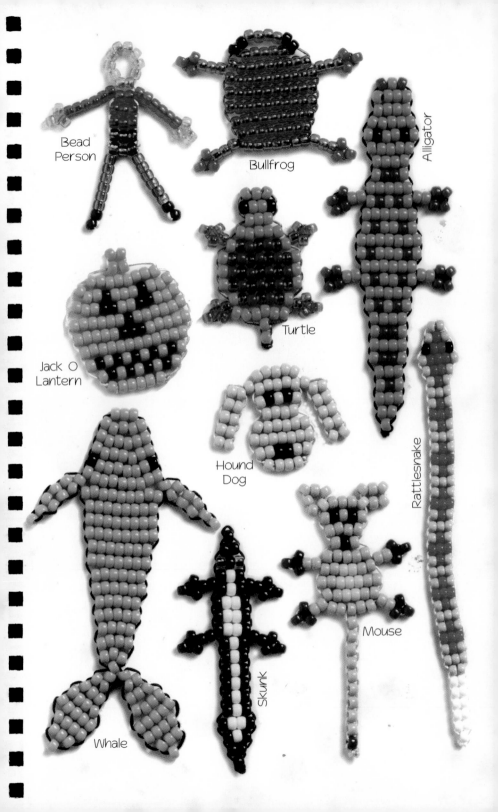

Bead Person

Bullfrog

Alligator

Jack O Lantern

Turtle

Hound Dog

Rattlesnake

Whale

Skunk

Mouse

Whale

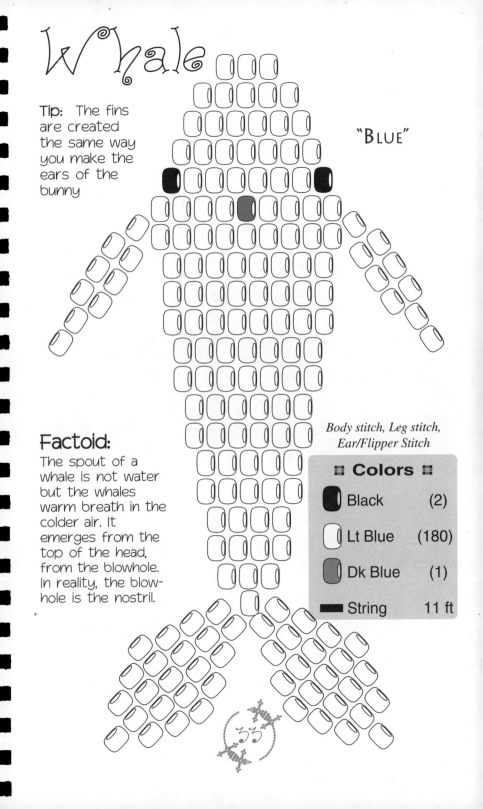

Tip: The fins are created the same way you make the ears of the bunny

"BLUE"

Factoid:

The spout of a whale is not water but the whales warm breath in the colder air. It emerges from the top of the head, from the blowhole. In reality, the blowhole is the nostril.

Body stitch, Leg stitch, Ear/Flipper Stitch

▪ Colors ▪

Black	(2)
Lt Blue	(180)
Dk Blue	(1)
String	11 ft

33

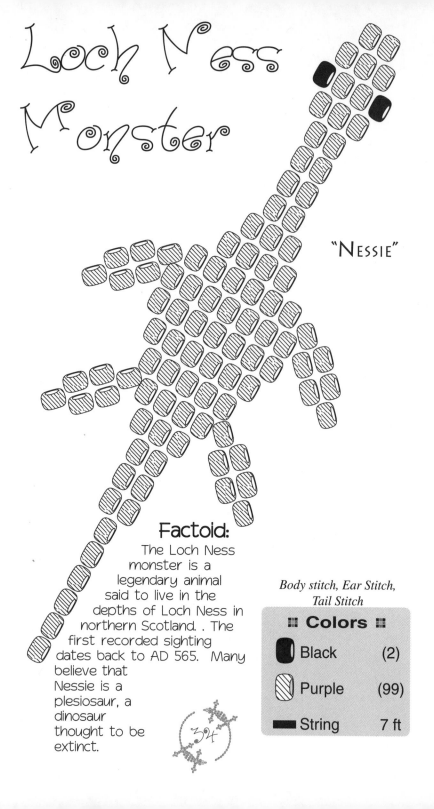

Loch Ness Monster

"NESSIE"

Factoid:
The Loch Ness monster is a legendary animal said to live in the depths of Loch Ness in northern Scotland. . The first recorded sighting dates back to AD 565. Many believe that Nessie is a plesiosaur, a dinosaur thought to be extinct.

Body stitch, Ear Stitch, Tail Stitch

∷ **Colors** ∷	
Black	(2)
Purple	(99)
String	7 ft

34

Penguin

"PENGO"

Factoid:

Penguins are found in the colder waters of oceans around southern South America and Africa, in Australia and New Zealand, and on many islands. Penguins are powerful swimmers sometimes reaching speeds of 25 m.p.h..

Body stitch, Ear/ Flipper Stitch

:: Colors ::		
Black	(38)
Yellow	(28)
White	(55)
String	8 ft

STEP 1

Start the penguin with the body stitch and work down to the flipper. Place 10 beads on side B of the string. (for more detailed instructions, see the Bunny)

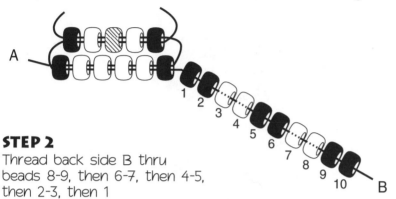

STEP 2

Thread back side B thru beads 8-9, then 6-7, then 4-5, then 2-3, then 1

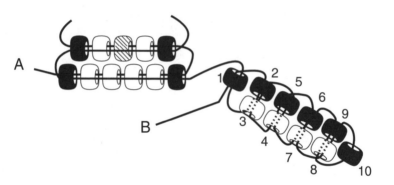

STEP 3

Continue with side A, Continue following the pattern until you reach the last row.

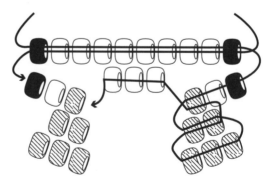

Duckie

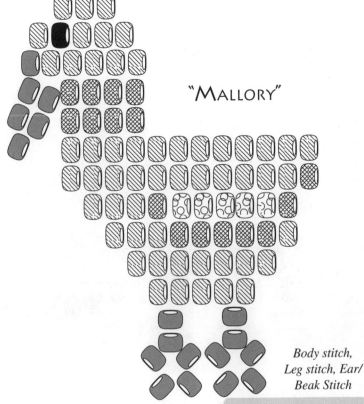

"MALLORY"

*Body stitch,
Leg stitch, Ear/
Beak Stitch*

Factoid:

Ducks waddle because their legs are placed far apart and usually well to the rear. The feathers of the male, or drake, can have striking color patterns that are sometimes iridescent. A duck's front toes are fully webbed for swimming and diving.

37

▮ Colors ▮

▮	Black	(1)
▮	Gold	(18)
▮	Yellow	(54)
▮	Green	(16)
▮	Lt Blue	(5)
▬	String	6 ft

STEP 1

Start the duckie with the body stitch and work down to the duck bill.

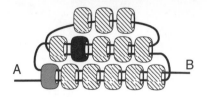

STEP 2

Using side **A** of your string thread thru 5 beads of the bill Order 1 - 2 - 3 - 4 - 5

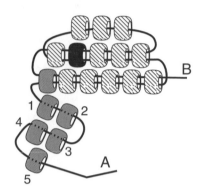

STEP 3

Continue with side **A** and thread back thru the same beads. Order 3 - 4 - 1 - 2

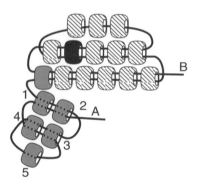

STEP 4

Using the layout create a body stitch with the next 4 beads

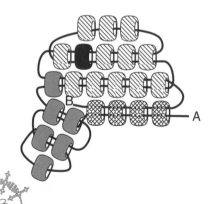

STEP 5

At the point where the body becomes long, pass side A through beads 1 - 12. Pass side B through beads 5-4-3-2-1

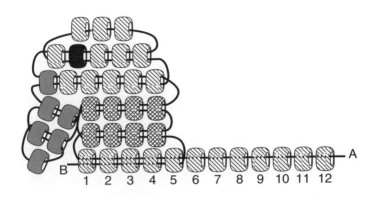

STEP 6

When making the feet. Place 1 body bead on side A. Complete one foot. Repeat on side B. When both feet are complete, add 3 bead body stitch between them.

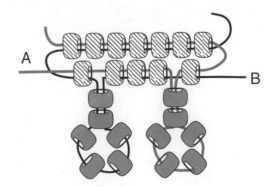

Chicken

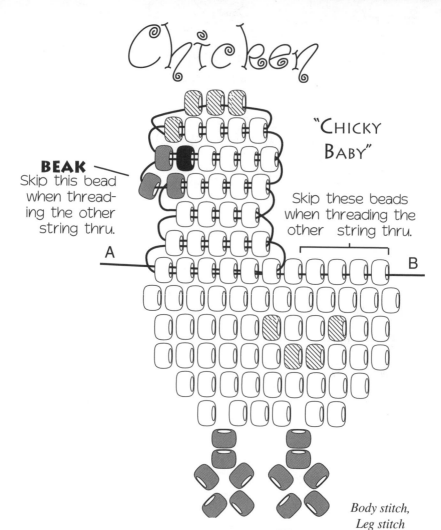

"CHICKY BABY"

BEAK —
Skip this bead when threading the other string thru.

Skip these beads when threading the other string thru.

A

B

Body stitch,
Leg stitch

Factoid:

The chicken, Gallus gallus or G. domesticus, is probably the most common bird in the world. The U.S. produces more than 68 billion eggs, about 500,000 billion eggs throughout the world. The rooster will fight for territory using bony outgrowths of the legs called spurs.

▦ Colors ▦	
◼ Black	(1)
◻ White	(71)
▨ Red	(9)
◼ Yellow	(14)
▬ String	6 ft

40

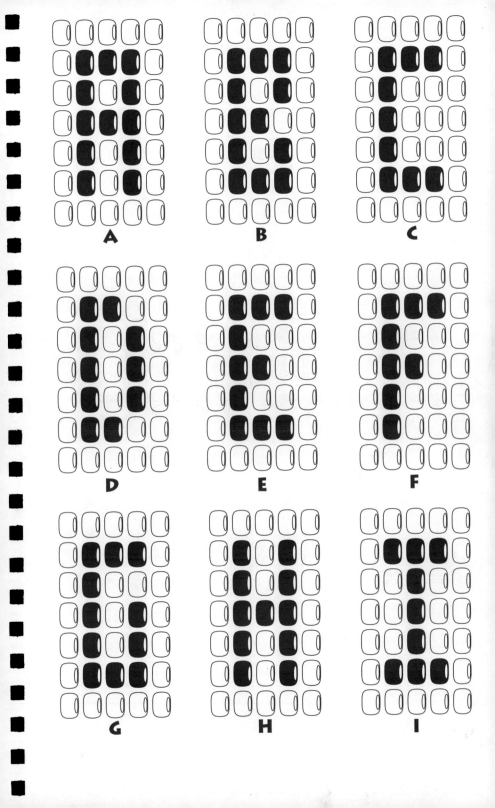

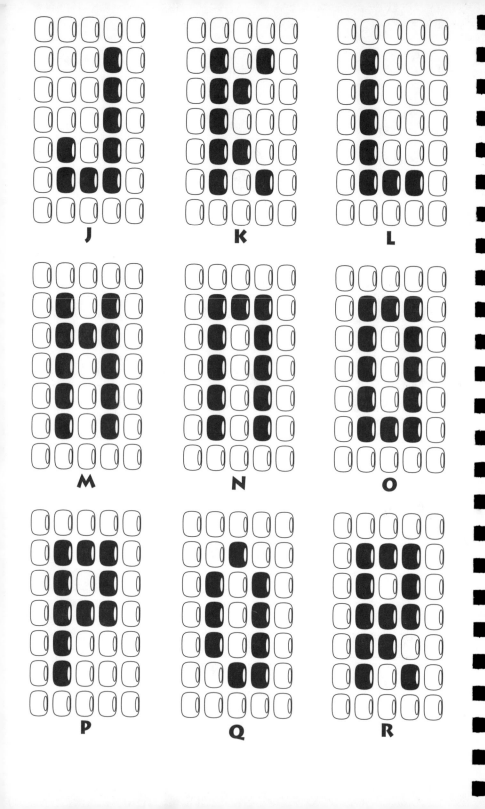

J

K

L

M

N

O

P

Q

R

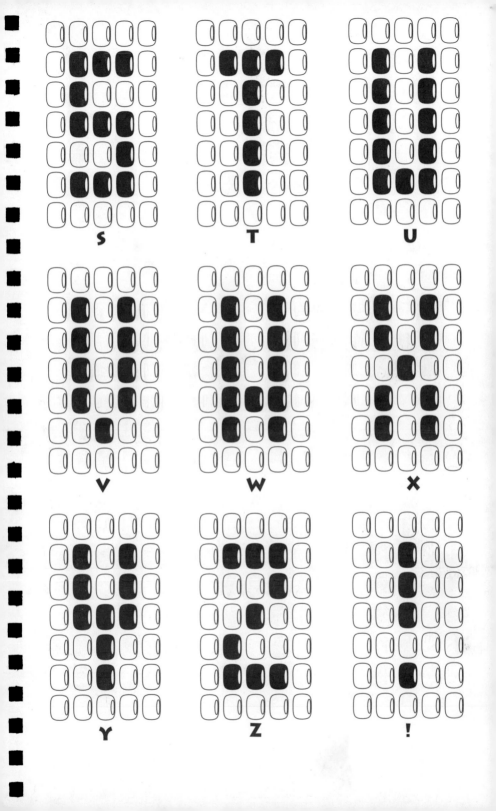

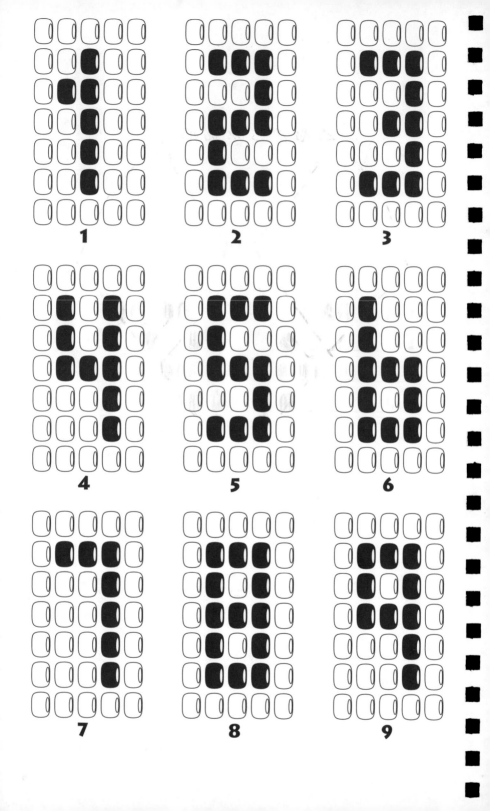

Design Your Own
Bead Animal
(Christmas Ornaments)

DESIGN SHEET

Gray Alien

DESIGN SHEET

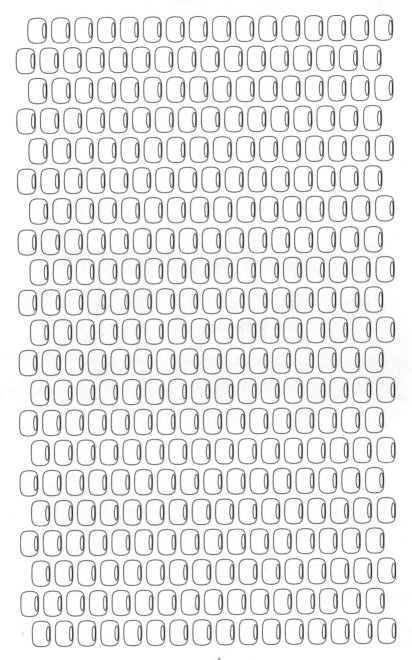

If you would like a list of other titles and forthcoming books from Bead Man Press, or need help locating additional copies, please contact us at:

Bead Man Press
1420 NW Gilman Blvd.
Box 2702
Issaquah, WA 98027

or visit our website: **www.thebeadman.com**